What Is My Shadow Made Of?

Questions Children Ask About Science

Written by Neil Morris
Illustrated by Mik Brown

JOSHUA MORRIS PUBLISHING

Contents

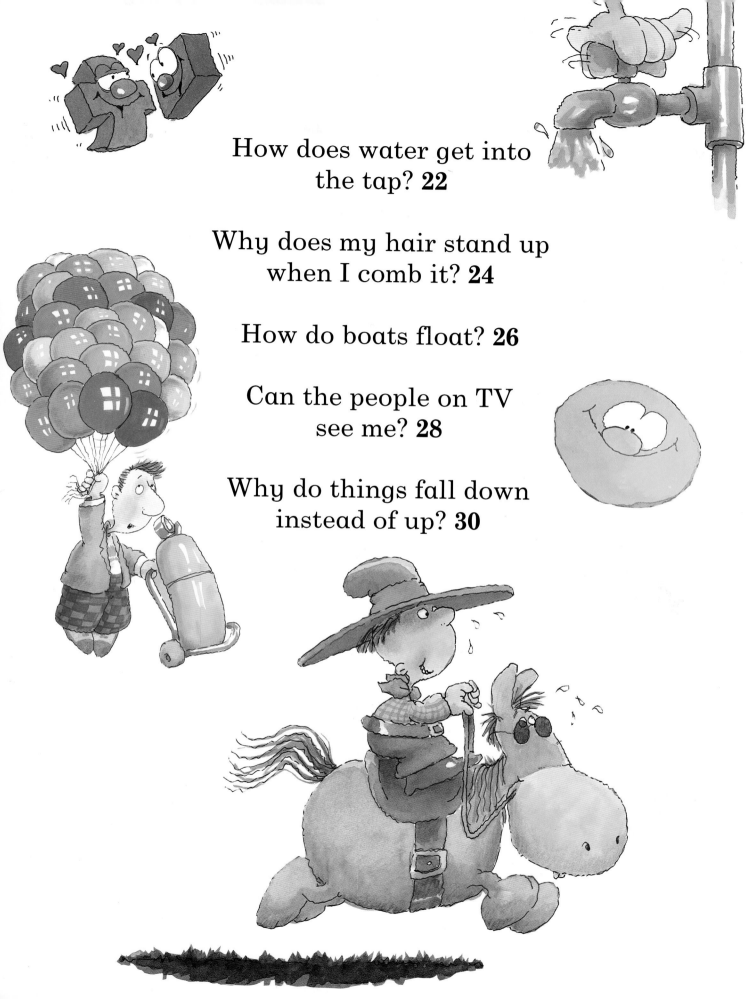

How does water get into the tap?

Why does my hair stand up when I comb it?

How do boats float?

Can the people on TV see me?

Why do things fall down instead of up?

Why do drums go boom?

All sounds, from big booms on a bass drum to zinging strings on a guitar, are made from vibrations — something shaking back and forth very quickly. When you hit a drum, the drum skin vibrates. When you strum a guitar, the strings vibrate.

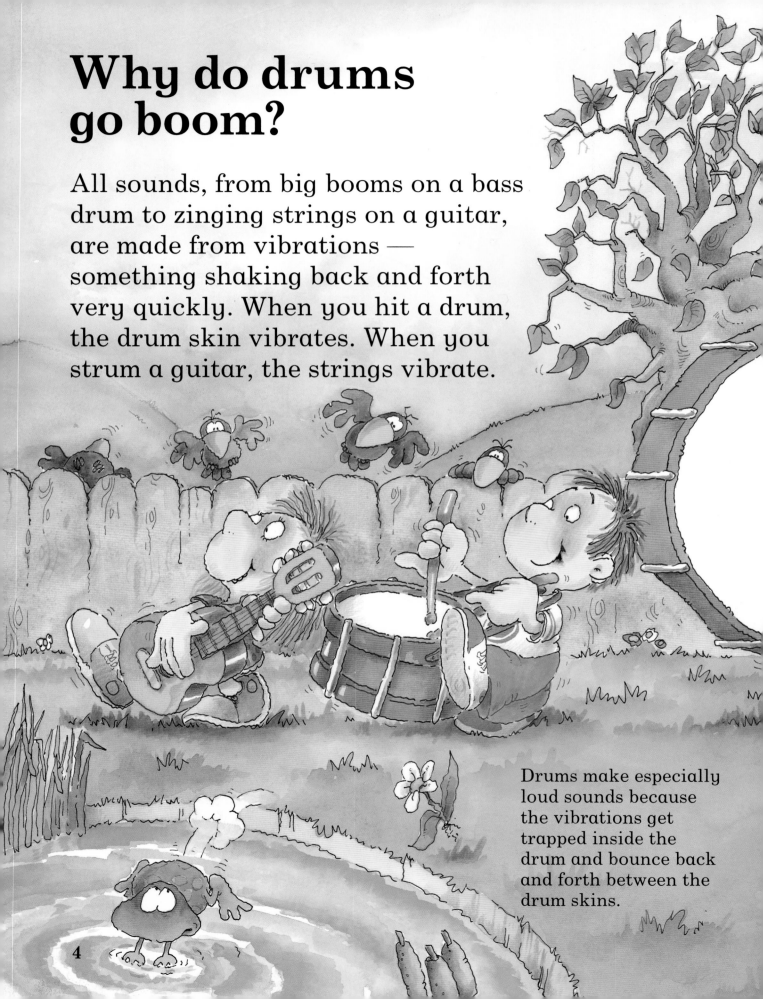

Drums make especially loud sounds because the vibrations get trapped inside the drum and bounce back and forth between the drum skins.

Inside your throat are vocal cords, which are like two rubber bands. They vibrate when you speak or sing. You can feel them vibrating if you rest your fingers on your throat and say something.

Try it yourself!
There's an easy way to see a drum making vibrations. Put some grains of rice on the top of the drum and then tap it gently. The vibrations make the rice dance and jump. If you hit the drum harder, some rice grains may jump right off!

What makes a car go?

When an adult turns the key in a car, the car's engine starts up. The engine turns the wheels and makes the car go by burning a mixture of petrol and air. Without the key, the engine, or the petrol, the car isn't going anywhere!

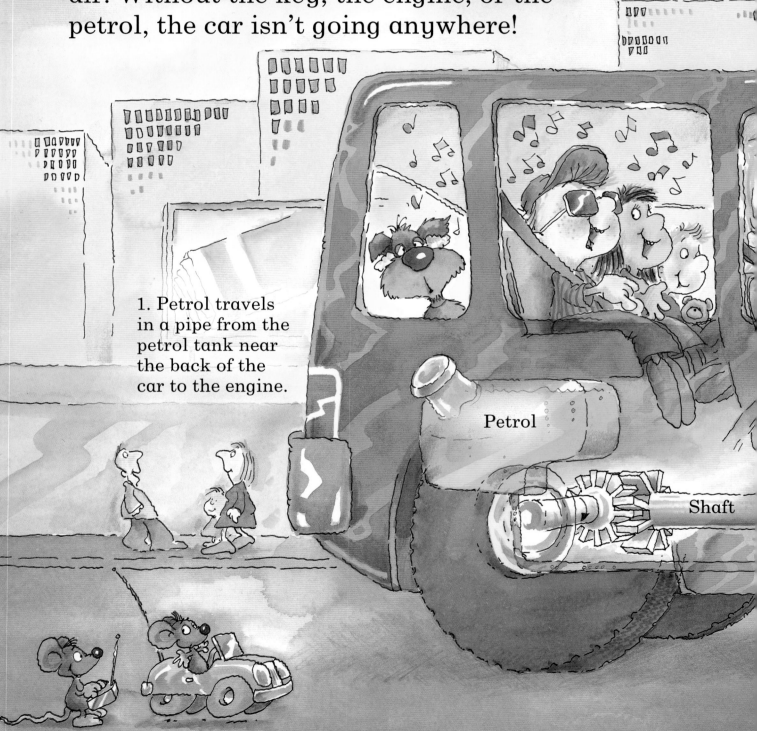

1. Petrol travels in a pipe from the petrol tank near the back of the car to the engine.

Petrol

Shaft

2. When the petrol reaches the engine, the petrol burns in a series of tiny explosions. These explosions push the pistons up and down. This movement turns a long shaft inside the car.

Engine

Piston

3. The turning shaft turns the wheels.

What is air?

Air is a mixture of invisible gases that is all around you. One of the gases in air is oxygen, which we all need to breathe. Although you can't see air, you can see what it does when you blow air into a balloon. You can feel air in a breeze and hear it when you blow a horn.

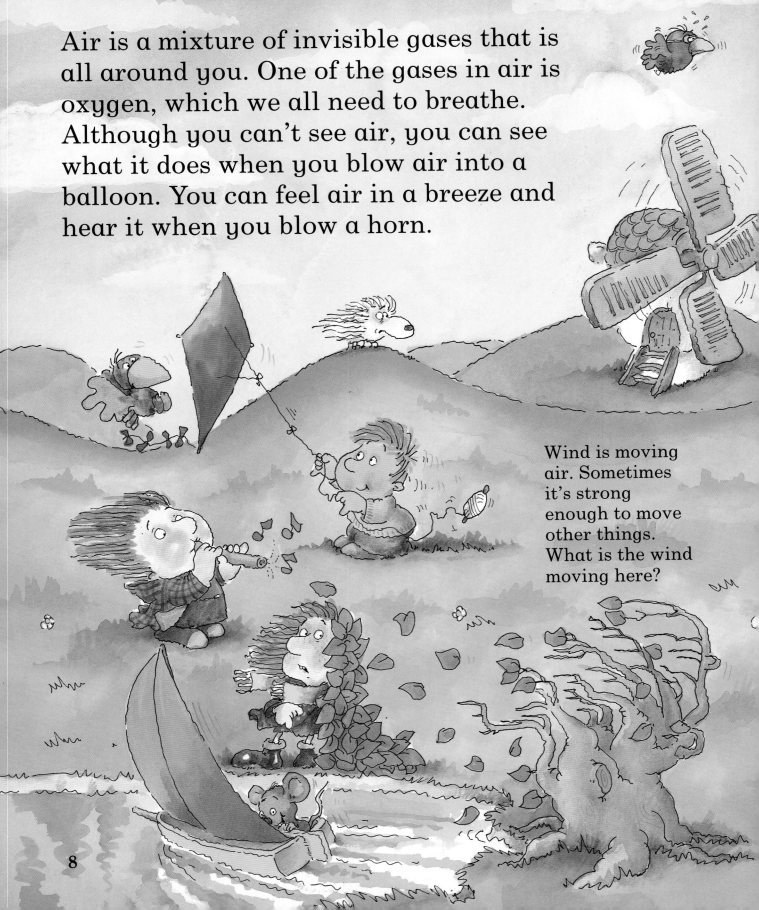

Wind is moving air. Sometimes it's strong enough to move other things. What is the wind moving here?

Helium balloons fly into the sky because helium is lighter than air.

Hot air is lighter than cold air. Some big balloons are filled with hot air and float up, up, and away!

If you blow up a balloon with air, it falls to the ground because air has weight.

If you were to put all the air in a big room into a balloon, the balloon would weigh about as much as a grown-up!

HELIUM

What is my shadow made of?

Your shadow isn't made of anything — it's just a dark shape. If you try to touch it, all you do is make a different shadow! Shadows are made when something gets in the way of light. So if you get in the path of sunlight, you block out the light and make a shadow.

At high noon, when the sun is directly overhead, the sunlight hits only the top of your body. You block out less light, so your shadow is smaller.

When the sun is low in the sky, your whole body blocks its path, so your shadow is longer.

Shadow pictures
A dark room, someone with a torch, and your own two hands are all you need to have fun making shadow pictures on the wall. Can you guess what each one of these will be? (Hint: All are animals!)

Try it yourself!
You can make your shadow get bigger and smaller. Hold a light so that you can see your shadow on a blank wall.

Move the light closer; then move it further away. What happens to your shadow?

Why does my magnet stick to some things?

Your magnet only sticks to things made of metal. And the metal must have iron or nickel in it. Keys and paper clips will stick to the magnet like magic. But things made of wood, plastic, glass, cloth, or rubber will not.

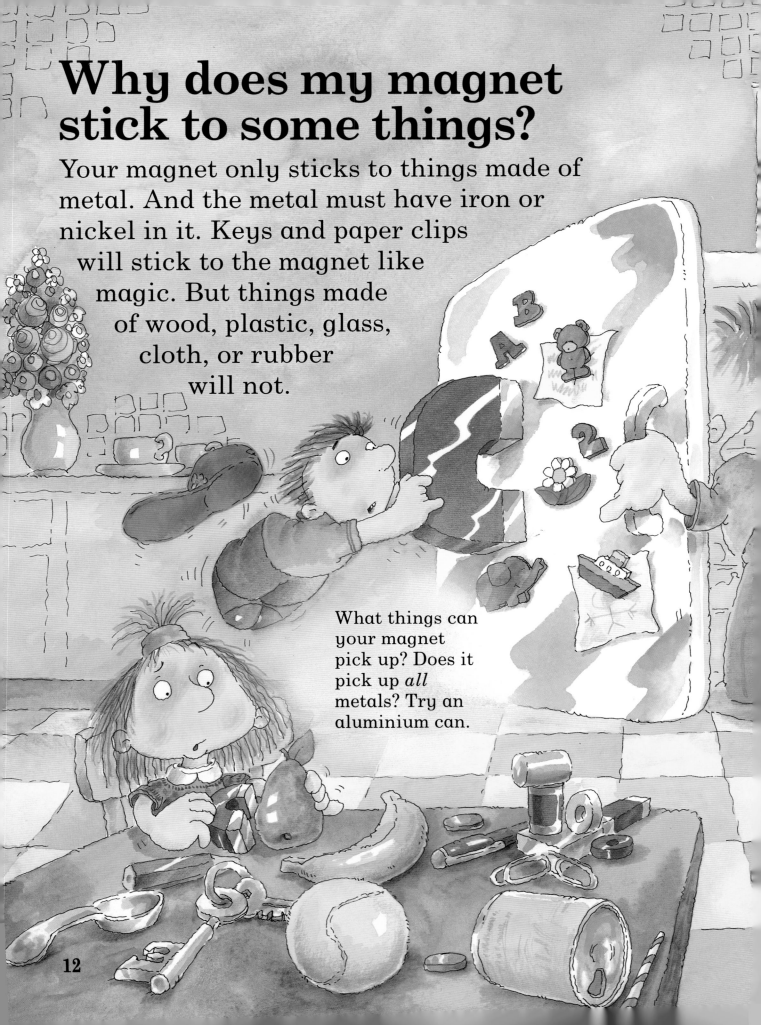

What things can your magnet pick up? Does it pick up *all* metals? Try an aluminium can.

Try it yourself!
The ends of magnets are called poles. Each magnet has a north pole on one end and a south pole on the other.

If you put two magnets with opposite poles near each other, they will pull together. If the same poles are together, the magnets push each other away.

Do you have magnets on your refrigerator? They stick to the door because the door is made of steel, which is a metal with iron in it.

Magnets can make metal things more magnetic. If you hold a paper clip against a magnet, the paper clip will then pick up more paper clips.

How do planes fly?

Planes can fly because they have high-speed engines and specially shaped wings that are curved on the top and flatter underneath. The wings work with the air currents to lift the plane into the sky and keep it there — until the pilot lands it.

Before the plane can take off into the air, it needs to go very fast to force air over the wings. That's why planes use powerful engines to speed down the runway.

Try it yourself!
You can see how a plane wing works by blowing hard across the top of a sheet of paper. The end of the sheet lifts into the air. This is because the air is moving faster over the top of the paper than below it.

Air rushes over and under the wings of a moving plane.

The air moving over the curved tops of the wings has further to go — so it moves faster and gets spread out more thinly. This reduces the air pressure pushing down on the tops of the wings, so the plane rises.

Why can I see myself in the mirror?

Because of the way light bounces off mirrors —
it's like the way a ball bounces off a wall.
When you look in a mirror, light first bounces
from you onto the shiny surface of the mirror.
Then it bounces back from the mirror to your
eyes, and you see yourself.
What you see is called
a reflection.

Light goes straight
through clear glass.
If you paint glass silver on
the back, light will bounce
back to you, creating a
reflection. This is how a
mirror works.

You can have fun
with mirrors because
they turn things around.
If you write your name on a
piece of paper and hold it up
in front of a mirror, the letters will
appear back to front in the mirror.

HALL OF MIRRORS

In a hall of mirrors, the mirrors are curved so that light doesn't bounce straight back. It bounces back in different directions, which changes the reflections.

If you stand between two mirrors that face each other, you'll see many reflections. This is because light keeps bouncing back and forth between the two mirrors, creating more and more yous!

How many colours are there?

Millions! From lemon yellow to sky blue to tree green, there are so many colours you can't count them all! That's because you can mix colours together to make new colours. How many colours can you make?

You need only three colours to make lots of other colours. The three main colours are red, yellow, and blue. They are called primary colours.

Colour mix-up
If you mix these paints, what colours will you get? Lift the flap to see.

19

What makes things slippery?

Things are slippery because their surfaces are smooth and they slide easily. Just think how slippery new party shoes can be. Trainers aren't slippery because their soles are rough and they grip any surface you walk on. The rough soles create friction — a force that stops things from sliding.

Friction is what allows you to grip the rope in a tug-of-war. Without it, the rope would slip right out of your hands!

Without friction, the bow you tied in your shoelace would slip out, and your shoe would slip off.

Try it yourself!

You can feel friction. Just rub your hands together. Friction makes heat.

Soap reduces friction. Wash your hands with soap, and see how they slide.

Like the bottoms of your trainers, tyres also have special marks that keep them from slipping.

When you squeeze bicycle brakes, friction between the brakes and the wheels makes your bike stop. Without friction, your bike would roll on forever.

21

How does water get into the tap?

It starts with rain. First, rain falls into lakes, rivers and reservoirs. Then it travels through tanks and pipes, being cleaned along the way. Finally, it is pumped through underground pipes into your home, ready at the turn of the tap.

1. Rain falls from clouds into streams and rivers that flow down to fill a big reservoir.

2. Then the water is cleaned. A chemical called alum is added, and dirt and sand are filtered out.

Why does my hair stand up when I comb it?

When you comb your hair quickly on a dry day, the comb rubs against the thousands of hairs on your head and makes a kind of electricity called static electricity. That electricity is what makes your hair stand up!

Positively shocking!

Opposites attract!

Static electricity can be positive (+) or negative (–).

Two positives push each other away.

Two negatives also push each other away.

But one positive and one negative attract each other!

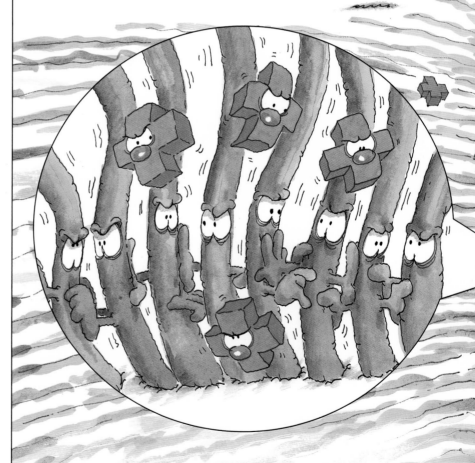

Combing your hair on a dry day gives all the hairs the same positive charge. Each hair tries to push the next one away. When all the hairs are pushing against each other, they all stand up.

Try it yourself!
Here's a magic trick
you can do with static
electricity. Rub a
balloon on a sweater to
give it a static charge.
Then put one hand on
top of the balloon.
Surprise! The balloon
will stick to your hand.
Can you tell why?

Have you ever seen little
sparks fly when you take
off a sweater in the dark?
This is static electricity
made by your clothes
rubbing together.

How do boats float?

Boats float because of their shape and weight. A boat's weight pushes it down, but the water pushes it up. The boat's weight is spread out over a large area, so the water has a lot to push against. This holds the boat up. But if the boat fills with water, it gets heavier and pushes down harder. Then the boat will sink.

Try it yourself!
Try floating a ball of clay. It sinks because all its weight is in a very small place. There's not much for the water to push against. If you take the same clay and make it into a boat shape, it will float.

The shape of a boat helps it push a lot of water out of the way. The water that is pushed away pushes back against the boat and holds it up.

What will float and what will sink?
Take a guess! What do you think?

A metal spoon

An apple

Coins

A sponge

Pebbles

A wooden spoon

27

Can the people on TV see me?

You can see them, but they can't see you! They are in a TV studio and all they can see are the cameras and crew. The camera tapes the show. Then the show is broadcast to your home. So when a funny clown says, "I'll see you next week!" what he means is, "You'll see *me* next week!"

2. The signals move along a wire to a transmitter. Each signal carries a piece of the picture.

1. The TV camera changes the clown's picture into electric signals.

3. At the transmitter, the signals are made stronger and sent out into the air.

4. The aerial on your roof picks up the signals and sends them down a wire to your TV set.

5. The TV changes the signals back into pictures and sound. On with the show!

Why do things fall down instead of up?

Because of gravity. Gravity is an invisible force that pulls everything on earth downwards. When you throw something up in the air, gravity soon pulls it back down. The moon has gravity too, but much less. Look at the difference gravity can make!

Thanks to gravity, there is only one way to go from the top of a slide — down.

When you throw a ball up, gravity is what brings it back down again.

You can bounce high on a trampoline, but you always come straight back down — because of gravity!

A slide on the moon wouldn't be much fun. You would slide down, but very slowly.

The moon has less gravity than earth because the moon is much smaller.

If you were on the moon and tossed a ball up, it would take a long time to come down because there's not much gravity pulling on it.

Imagine a trampoline on the moon. You would bounce six times as high as you do on earth.

Published 1995 by Joshua Morris Publishing, a division
of The Reader's Digest Association, Inc, 4 North Parade,
Bath, BA1 1LF
Produced by Larousse plc

Copyright © 1994 Larousse plc

ISBN 1 - 85724 - 072 - 3

**British Library Cataloguing-in-Publication Data.
A catalogue record for this book is available from
the British Library.**

Printed in Hong Kong